I0841346

Time: The Most Important Resource You Have

Welcome to "Precious Time: Strategies for Effective Management." In an increasingly fast-paced world, where time seems to slip through our fingers, it has become essential to learn how to manage it intelligently and skillfully.

This book is much more than just a guide to time management; it is a profound journey into how we can master the most precious asset we have: our time.

Chapter 1: The Importance of Time

We begin this journey by examining the importance of time in our daily lives. Time is the most valuable asset we possess, and it is a resource that, once spent, cannot be recovered. Understanding how fundamental time is is the first step towards effective management.

We will also explore the perception of time since our feeling of "lack of time" is often tied to our subjective perception.

Chapter 2: Defining the Concept of Time

To understand how to manage time, we must first define what time is. We will examine various philosophical and scientific definitions of time, exploring concepts such as linear time, cyclic time, and the subjective experience of time.

This understanding will help us view time from different perspectives and better adapt to its challenges.

Chapter 3: Identifying Priorities

One of the keys to effective time management is the ability to set priorities.

Here, we will explore how to establish clear goals and use the Eisenhower Matrix for activity prioritization.

We will learn to distinguish between what is urgent and what is important, helping us focus our energy on tasks that have a significant impact on our lives.

Chapter 4: Effective Planning

Now that we know what is important, let's move on to the planning phase. We will explore time planning methods, from using traditional agendas to adopting digital tools.

We will learn the art of creating a daily or weekly plan and discover available tools to simplify this crucial activity.

Chapter 5: Managing Distractions

Life is full of distractions that can steal precious time. In this chapter, we will identify the main sources of distraction and discuss strategies to reduce them.

We will explore the concept of concentration and flow, learning how to maintain focus on important tasks without falling into the traps of modern distractions.

Chapter 6: Delegation and Collaboration

No one can do everything alone. We will discover the art of delegation and how to collaborate effectively with others.

We will also examine modern tools that facilitate teamwork and the assignment of responsibilities.

Chapter 7: Optimizing Personal Productivity

Personal productivity is a constant challenge, but with the right time management techniques, we can significantly increase our efficiency.

We will explore techniques for managing time to maximize productivity.

We will discover the 2-minute rule and strategies to avoid procrastination.

Chapter 8: Stress Management and Work-Life Balance

Time must be managed not only for productivity but also for well-being.

We will recognize and address stress, learning to find a healthy balance between work and personal life.

We will explore relaxation and stress management techniques that will help us stay calm even in the busiest moments.

Chapter 9: Measuring and Evaluating Progress

The importance of measuring results cannot be underestimated. In this chapter, we will examine how to assess our use of time and adjust our planning based on results.

We will learn to use key performance indicators and tools to measure our progress.

Chapter 10: Advanced Time Management Strategies

At this point, we will be ready to explore advanced time management techniques.

We will discuss how to manage time in complex situations and adapt to periods of change.

We will also explore long-term time management and how to plan for the future.

Chapter 11: Time Management in Challenging Situations

This chapter will address the art of managing time in difficult moments.

You can start by sharing stories of people who have faced stressful or crisis situations and how they managed their time in such moments. Explore the following areas:

- How to Stay Focused and Productive: Share strategies and techniques for maintaining focus during stressful situations, such as breaking tasks into more manageable steps or using breathing techniques.

- Managing Stress and Frustration: Provide advice on how to recognize and cope with stress and frustration constructively. You can introduce stress management techniques like meditation or physical exercise.

- Adapting Planning to Circumstances: Explain how it's important to be flexible in planning during difficult situations and how to adapt your goals and priorities to the situation.

Chapter 12: Time Management for Teams and Projects

This chapter will focus on time management in a team or project context.

You can start by presenting the value of time management in these contexts and then explore the following areas:

- Defining Priorities and Roles: Explain how to establish clear priorities within a team and assign specific roles to each member to ensure effective workload distribution.

- Planning and Coordination: Introduce specific planning methods for projects and how to coordinate the team's activities to achieve objectives.

- Monitoring and Evaluation: Illustrate how to constantly monitor project progress and evaluate achieved results. You could introduce tools like Gantt charts or project management software.

Chapter 13: Time Management for Personal Life

This chapter will explore the application of time management techniques to personal life.

Begin by showing how good time management can improve the quality of life and then explore the following areas:

- Work-Life Balance: Offer advice on how to balance work with personal interests, hobbies, and leisure time.

- Time Management for Recreational and Relaxation Activities: Describe how to plan time for activities that bring joy and relaxation, such as hobbies, reading, or sports.

- Planning Family and Social Commitments: Explain the importance of planning family and social commitments to maintain healthy and fulfilling relationships.

Chapter 14: Time Management for Learning and Growth

In this chapter, we explore how time management can optimize learning and personal development.

We discuss the importance of setting SMART goals, finding time for study, and applying acquired knowledge.

Chapter 15: Time Management for Health and Well-being

This chapter addresses how to use time management to improve physical and mental health.

We examine defining health goals, integrating healthy habits into daily routines, and managing stress and anxiety through effective planning.

Chapter 16:Time Management for Long-Term Goals

Time management extends beyond daily life and can be applied to long-term goals.

In this chapter, we explore how to set realistic and meaningful long-term goals.

We learn to break these goals into short-term objectives, creating a clear path to long-term success.

We also discuss how to monitor and evaluate progress toward these goals, ensuring we stay on track and maintain motivation over time.

Time management becomes a powerful tool for transforming long-term dreams into concrete, planned, and achievable realities.

Appendix

Useful Resources For those wishing to delve deeper into the topic of time management, we will provide a list of books, websites, and useful tools.

These resources will help readers continue their learning journey and find further inspiration for increasingly effective time management.

This book is destined to become your trusted companion in the challenge of time management.

Prepare to embark on a journey toward personal success and well-being, learning to master your time and create a life that fills you with satisfaction.

Chapter 1

"Every moment we spend is an irreplaceable resource. Learn to value your time, and you will have the power to shape your future"

The Importance of Time Management in Daily Life

Time is one of the most precious assets we have in life. It is a limited, invaluable, and unrecoverable resource. Every day, we receive a fixed allocation of time, and how we choose to use it can have a significant impact on our quality of life, both personally and professionally. Time management is the art of using this precious asset efficiently and effectively.

To fully understand the importance of time management in daily life, it is essential to reflect on how our time influences various aspects of our existence. Let's explore how time management impacts different spheres:

Productivity and Goal Achievement Time management is closely linked to our productivity and our ability to achieve the goals we have set for ourselves. When we manage time inefficiently, we tend to waste time on non-essential activities, delaying progress toward our objectives. On the other hand, careful planning and judicious allocation of time resources allow us to take significant steps towards achieving our goals.

Stress Reduction Poor time utilization often leads to stress. The constant race against time, a lack of time to complete tasks, and an accumulation of deadlines can generate unsustainable stress and pressure. Conscious time management helps reduce stress levels by allowing us to plan ahead, face challenges more organized, and maintain a sense of control over our lives.

Work-Life Balance Balancing work and personal life is a crucial aspect of overall well-being. Poor time management can lead to excessive dedication to work at the expense of family life, hobbies, and relaxation. On the other hand, effective time management enables us to allocate time for both spheres, ensuring a balanced and fulfilling life.

Growth Opportunities In the professional context, time management can directly influence growth and career advancement opportunities. Individuals who demonstrate effective time management are often considered valuable assets by companies. The ability to meet deadlines, be punctual, and efficiently complete projects can lead to promotions and greater recognition in the workplace.

Quality of Relationships Even our personal relationships benefit from time management. When we dedicate quality time to family and friends, we strengthen emotional bonds and create precious memories. Time management allows us to be emotionally present in relationships, which is essential for their growth and longevity.

Self-Growth and Continuous Learning Finally, time management promotes self-growth and continuous learning. When we use our time to acquire new skills, read, study, or pursue stimulating hobbies, we invest in ourselves.

This process of self-growth contributes to our personal development and enriches our lives.

In conclusion, the importance of time management in daily life is undeniable. This skill not only enhances our productivity and reduces stress but also impacts virtually every aspect of our existence. Throughout this book, we will explore in-depth how to develop time management skills and apply them practically to improve our daily lives. Keep reading to discover strategies and techniques to maximize your time and achieve meaningful results.

Chapter 2

"Those who fully grasp the value of time possess the key to unlock the doors of efficiency and success."

Definition of the Concept of Tme

Time is one of the most fascinating and complex entities that humanity has ever known.

In simple terms, time is a dimension in which events occur sequentially, creating the sensation of past, present, and future. It is an inexorable flow that governs our existence and influences every aspect of life on Earth. However, its nature and significance go far beyond this basic definition. At its deepest essence, time is a measure of existence itself. It is the context in which everything that exists takes shape and evolves. Time is the canvas on which we paint our experiences, an endless journey where our stories intertwine with those of others. It is an invaluable asset that, once spent, cannot be recovered.

Perception of Time

The perception of time is an intriguing facet of our relationship with this dimension. Each individual has a personal perception of time influenced by factors such as age, culture, life experiences, and personal situations. Time can seem to fly when we're having fun and engaging in stimulating activities, while it can drag slowly when facing difficult or boring moments.

The perception of time is relative, and this concept has been extensively studied in Einstein's theory of relativity.

This means that time can be perceived differently from individual to individual and in different circumstances.

This subjectivity makes time an extraordinary element of our existence, capable of bending to our experiences and emotions.

Its Importance in Our Lives

The importance of time in our lives is immeasurable. Time is the most precious asset we possess, and how we use it directly influences our quality of life. It is a limited resource, yet we often find ourselves wasting it unconsciously, unaware of its intrinsic value.

Time offers us the opportunity to learn, grow, create, love, and pursue our dreams.

It is the fabric with which we build our future and reflect on our past. Its significance becomes evident when we reflect on how much time we dedicate to things that do not truly enrich or fulfill us.

Conscious time management is essential to maximize the use of this limited resource. By learning to understand time, perceive it more consciously, and value it, we can transform it into a valuable ally for a more satisfying and meaningful life.

In the following chapters, we will explore methods and strategies to make the most of our relationship with time and achieve greater personal fulfillment.

Chapter 3

" Setting priorities doesn't mean saying yes to everything, but saying yes to

what matters most. "

Identifying Priorities

The Importance of Setting Goals

One of the fundamental pillars of effective time management is the ability

to set clear and well-defined goals.

Goals are like stars in the night sky; they guide us, inspire us, and help us give meaning and direction to our lives.

Without goals, time can slip away without a specific purpose, leaving us with a sense of emptiness and dissatisfaction.

Goals can be short-term or long-term, personal or professional. They can relate to self-improvement, career, relationships, or any other area of life.

The key to setting effective goals is to make them S.M.A.R.T.: Specific, Measurable, Achievable, Realistic, and Time-bound.

This approach helps us clearly define what we want to achieve and create a concrete plan to do so.

Once goals are established, they become the compass guiding our daily decisions.

They help us focus on what truly matters and avoid unnecessary distractions.

Goals motivate us to make the most of our time and resources to get closer and closer to their realization.

The Eisenhower Matrix for Activity Prioritization

Once goals are established, the next step is to learn how to prioritize activities based on how much they contribute to the achievement of those goals. The Eisenhower Matrix is a powerful and widely used prioritization tool that can assist us in this process.

This matrix categorizes activities based on two fundamental criteria: urgency and importance. Each activity can be placed in one of four categories:

1. Urgent and Important: These are top-priority activities. They require our immediate attention and align with our goals. For example, resolving a work crisis or addressing a health issue.

2. Important but Not Urgent: These activities are crucial for long-term goal achievement. However, they do not require an immediate response. This includes strategic planning, training, and personal improvement.

3. Urgent but Not Important: These activities often distract us from achieving our goals. They are pressing but do not significantly contribute to our long-term success. For example, responding to non-important phone calls or handling non-critical interruptions.

4. Neither Urgent nor Important: These activities are pure time-wasters and should be avoided or minimized. They include futile tasks, time drains, and valueless distractions.

Learning to use the Eisenhower Matrix allows us to focus our energy on high-importance tasks and reduce time spent on non-urgent or non-important matters. This approach helps us become more effective, achieve meaningful results, and manage our time more consciously.

In the next chapter, we will explore practical methods for planning and implementing these priorities.

Chapter 4

" Good planning is like the map that guides the traveler through the unfamiliar territory of time, allowing them to reach their desired destinations with precision and safety."

Time Planning Methods

Time planning is a crucial skill for effectively managing our life and work.

There are various methods and approaches that can help us structure our

time productively.

Some of the most common methods include:

- To-Do Lists: This is one of the simplest and most effective methods. We write a list of tasks we need to complete during the day and organize them by priority. This allows us to have a clear overview of our responsibilities and focus on the most important tasks.

- Online Calendar: Using a digital calendar like Google Calendar or Outlook can help plan commitments efficiently. You can set reminders and notifications to not forget important appointments or deadlines.

- Time Matrix: This method divides time into categories such as "urgency" and "importance" to determine how to allocate time to different activities. It helps identify high-priority tasks and avoid wasting time on less relevant things.

The Importance of a Daily or Weekly Plan

Short-term planning is just as crucial as long-term planning. A daily or weekly plan allows us to translate long-term goals into concrete actions.

Here's why it's important:

- Provides Structure: A daily or weekly plan creates structure for our time. It helps us organize activities consistently and avoid confusion.

- Enhances Productivity: Planning allows us to allocate time to specific tasks based on priorities. This increases productivity because we are less likely to waste time on less important activities.

- Maintains Focus: With a plan in hand, we are more likely to stick to our scheduled activities. This helps us stay focused and avoid distractions.

Tools for Planning

In the digital age, we have access to a wide range of tools and applications that simplify time planning. Some common tools include:

- Time Management Apps: Apps like Trello, Asana, or Notion allow you to organize projects and tasks effectively. They offer features for team collaboration and task delegation.

- Calendar Apps: As mentioned earlier, digital calendar apps make scheduling appointments and deadlines easier.

- To-Do List Apps: Apps like Todoist or Wunderlist are ideal for creating and managing to-do lists in an organized manner.

- Notification Tools: Tools like Slack or Microsoft Teams provide real-time notifications for team communication and collaboration.

In conclusion, time planning is a fundamental element for personal and professional success.

By using appropriate planning methods and suitable tools, we can optimize our use of time and achieve our goals more efficiently.

In the next chapter, we will explore further strategies for managing distractions and improving concentration.

Chapter 5

" Concentration is the key to unlock the door of success, while distraction management is the lock that keeps it closed."

Managing Distractions

Identifying the Main Sources of Distraction

In our modern world, we are constantly surrounded by a myriad of

distractions.

From digital devices that keep us connected 24/7 to the constant noise in the workplace, it's easy to lose focus.

The first step in addressing the issue of distractions is to identify them. Take some time to reflect on your days and pinpoint the situations or activities that take you away from important work.

These could be social media notifications, non-urgent phone calls, or even office chatter. Once you've identified these sources of distraction, you'll be able to address them more effectively.

Strategies to Reduce Distractions

Once you've identified the main sources of distraction in your life, it's time to develop strategies to reduce them.

This may involve turning off non-essential notifications on your phone during work hours or creating a quiet work environment where you can focus without interruptions.

You might also consider scheduling specific times to handle activities that would typically distract you, so you don't disrupt your workflow.

Concentration and Flow

Concentration is one of the most valuable skills you can develop in time management.

When you can fully concentrate on a single task, you become more productive and capable of achieving high-quality results.

The concept of 'flow' refers to a mental state where you are so immersed in a task that time seems to stand still.

To reach this state, it's important to minimize distractions and create an optimal work environment.

In the next chapter, we'll explore additional strategies to enhance your concentration and make the most of your time.

Concentration is the key to unlocking the door to success, while managing distractions is the lock that keeps it closed.

Chapter 6

" In the dance of productivity, delegation is the step that allows you to dance to the rhythm of success, while collaboration is the symphony that makes the performance extraordinary.."

Delegating and Collaborating

The art of delegation

Delegation is a fundamental skill in time management and leadership.

Knowing when and how to delegate tasks is a sign of professional maturity

and is essential for increasing your productivity.

Learning the art of delegation doesn't simply mean assigning tasks to someone else and forgetting about them, but rather understanding the strengths and skills of each team member to distribute responsibilities effectively.

In the next section, we will explore the key steps to becoming a master of the art of delegation.

How to Collaborate Effectively with Others

Collaboration is the lifeblood of any successful team. Learning to work effectively with others can lead to extraordinary results. But collaboration isn't just about sharing workspace or attending meetings. It's about creating an environment where ideas can flow freely, and where each team member feels valued and heard. In the next section, we will explore strategies to improve your collaboration skills and lead your team to success.

Tools for Teamwork Management

In today's digital world, there are a myriad of tools and technologies available to enhance teamwork management.

From project management applications to online communication platforms, these resources can simplify collaboration and increase team efficiency.

In the next section, we will examine some of the best tools available and how to use them effectively to manage teamwork.

Delegation is like conducting an orchestra: you need the right people, the right tools, and the right direction to create a harmonious melody of success.

Examples of Delegation

Imagine you are the head of an important project at the office. You have many responsibilities and deadlines to meet, but you know your colleague Maria is an expert in data analysis.

You decide to delegate the research and analysis part of the project to her. This allows you to focus on project planning and management tasks while Maria conducts research accurately and promptly.

Thanks to delegation, the project progresses smoothly, and you've saved valuable time.

Examples of Effective Collaboration

Suppose you are part of a marketing team. You have an important product launch coming up, and you need to create a comprehensive advertising campaign. You organize brainstorming meetings where everyone has the opportunity to share ideas. Thanks to this open collaboration, creative concepts and innovative marketing strategies emerge that no one could have developed alone. Effective collaboration allows your team to create a successful advertising campaign that captures the attention of your target audience.

Examples of Teamwork Management Tools

In your software development team, you use an online project management tool like Trello.

Each team member can view assigned tasks, track progress, and collaborate on project management.

Thanks to Trello, your team saves time in communication and planning, and everyone is always updated on ongoing activities.

Smart use of delegation, effective collaboration, and teamwork management tools can make a difference in your productivity and the success of your daily work.

Chapter 7

"Time management is the key to unlocking the door to productivity. Navigate wisely through the tides of your tasks and let time flow towards success."

Time Management Techniques to Increase Productivity

Time management is fundamental to becoming more productive and achieving significant results in your daily activities.

There are many techniques and strategies you can adopt to maximize your time and work efficiency.

One of the most effective is the Pomodoro Technique, created by Francesco Cirillo in the 1980s. This approach is based on well-defined work cycles, known as "pomodoros," each lasting 25 minutes, followed by a short 5-minute break. During each pomodoro, you focus exclusively on a single task, avoiding distractions.

This intermittent work cycle helps maintain concentration, boost productivity, and prevent mental fatigue.

Another crucial aspect of time management is goal-based planning. Defining clear and well-defined goals allows you to set priorities and focus on tasks that contribute most to your success.

For example, if your goal is to complete an important project by a deadline, you can plan the necessary tasks to achieve that goal and allocate the time and resources required.

This helps you avoid wasting time on secondary tasks and keeps your focus on the most relevant activities.

Task list management is another essential practice for increasing productivity. Keeping track of all your tasks and responsibilities in an organized list provides you with a clear overview of what needs to be done.

You can categorize your tasks, set deadlines, and prioritize to ensure you concentrate on the most important activities. Using digital tools like task management apps or software can further simplify this process.

Imagine being a university student with a series of exams to prepare for, assignments to complete, and a social life to maintain. Your day is already quite busy, but you want to improve your productivity to tackle all these challenges. Here's how you can apply some time management techniques:

1. Pomodoro Technique: Decide to use the Pomodoro Technique to focus better during study sessions. Set a timer for 25 minutes of concentrated study (the "pomodoro"), followed by a 5-minute break. Repeat this cycle. It allows you to maintain attention and avoid mental fatigue.

2. **Goal-Based Planning**: Before starting to study, clearly establish the goals you want to achieve during that study session. For example, you might decide to cover a specific chapter in your textbook or solve a certain number of problems. This provides you with a clear direction.

3. **Task List Management**: Keep a list of tasks to be done. Divide tasks into categories like "study," "assignments," "appointments," etc. Use tools like task management apps or a simple notebook to keep track of what you need to do.

4. **Goal Prioritization**: Use the Eisenhower Matrix to classify tasks based on importance and urgency. This will help you focus on critical tasks and avoid wasting time on less important matters.

5. **Eliminating Distractions**: When you study, turn off your phone or use distraction-blocking apps to avoid getting caught up in social media or unrelated activities. Concentration will help you study more efficiently.

6. **Time Management between Activities**: Don't overload your day. Schedule breaks between activities to rest your mind and recharge.

7. Celebrating Successes: At the end of the day, take a moment to reflect on what you've achieved. Celebrate your successes, even if they are small. This will give you extra motivation to continue being productive.

By adopting these techniques, you can manage your time more effectively, increase your productivity, and find the right balance between studying, working, and socializing.

The 2-Minute Rule

The 2-minute rule is a simple yet powerful strategy for efficiently handling small daily tasks. It's based on the idea that if you have a task that will take less than 2 minutes to complete, you should do it immediately instead of postponing it.

For example, responding to a short email, tidying up your desk, or making a quick phone call can all be completed in less than 2 minutes. By applying this rule, you can prevent small tasks from accumulating over time and becoming a source of stress.

Keeping a list of these quick tasks to do can help you make the most of free moments between appointments and commitments.

Imagine you're at work, deeply engrossed in your task. You're working on an important report when you suddenly notice that the plant on your desk is wilting and needs some water. Initially, you might be tempted to ignore the plant and continue working on the report. However, you remember the 2-minute rule.

According to this rule, you should immediately address tasks that take less than 2 minutes to complete. So, you set aside your work for a moment, grab the water jug you always keep handy, and water the plant. In less than 2 minutes, you've provided the plant with what it needed and returned to your work without feeling guilty or concerned about the withering plant.

This example illustrates how the 2-minute rule can be applied to everyday and seemingly insignificant situations.

By quickly addressing these small tasks, you avoid letting them accumulate over time and become a source of distraction or stress.

Additionally, by keeping your workspace or environment tidy and well-managed, you create a more pleasant and productive setting for yourself.

Strategies to Avoid Procrastination

Procrastination is a common adversary in time management and can hinder your productivity. To overcome this obstacle, it's essential to adopt effective strategies.

One of these is advance task planning. Before starting your workday, take the time to plan the activities that need to be completed. Set clear goals and allocate specific times for each task. This will give you a clear direction to follow throughout the day and reduce the temptation to procrastinate.

Another strategy is creating artificial deadlines for yourself. Setting personal deadlines for tasks helps maintain a sense of urgency and encourages consistent progress. For example, if you have a project due in a week, you could set a personal deadline to complete it in four days, leaving room for any revisions or improvements.

Finally, breaking complex tasks into smaller, manageable ones can help you avoid procrastination.

Often, the fear of tackling a daunting task can lead to procrastination.

However, by breaking the task into smaller, focused steps, it becomes easier to approach gradually. You can then tackle each step with more confidence and success.

These are just a few of the strategies and techniques you can use to improve your time management and increase your productivity.

Each of these practices is designed to help you make the most of your time and achieve your goals more efficiently.

Chapter 8

" Seek the balance between work and personal life, for it is in this balance

that you will find your true wealth."

Stress Management and Work-Life Balance

Stress Management and Work-Life Balance Identification of Stress

Recognizing stress is the first step in dealing with it effectively.

In this section, you will learn to identify the signs of stress in your body

and mind. From muscle tension to emotional changes, you will discover

how your body reacts to stress and how to identify stressful situations.

Causes of Stress To address stress, it is essential to understand its causes. We will explore the various sources of stress in daily life, from the work environment to personal challenges.

You will learn to identify what triggers your stress so you can develop specific strategies to address it. Dealing with Stress Dealing with stress requires a targeted approach.

In this section, we will examine different techniques for managing stress. From managing emotions to progressive muscle relaxation, you will discover how to deal with stress in a healthy and effective way. You will be able to develop a customized toolkit for managing stressful situations. Finding a Balance Between Work and Personal Life

The Importance of Balance

Balancing work and personal life is crucial for overall well-being. In this section, we will explore why finding this balance is so crucial. You will discover how excessive work can negatively impact your mental and physical health and learn the importance of dedicating time to your personal life.

Time Planning for Balance To find a balance between work and personal life, proper planning is necessary. We will examine practical strategies for planning your time so you can allocate space for both work-related and personal activities. You will learn to set boundaries and protect your personal time.

Creating a Balanced Environment The environment in which you live and work can significantly impact the balance between work and personal life.

We will explore how to create an environment that supports your well-being and promotes a better balance between these two spheres. From space management to decluttering, you will discover how to improve your environment to reduce stress. Relaxation and Stress Management Techniques

Importance of Relaxation Relaxation is an essential part of stress management.

In this section, we will explore the importance of relaxation for mental and physical well-being. You will learn how relaxation can help you rejuvenate your body and mind. Relaxation Techniques We will examine a range of relaxation techniques that you can incorporate into your daily routine. From meditation to deep breathing, you will discover how these techniques can help you manage stress effectively.

You will be able to choose the techniques that best suit your needs and lifestyle. Integrating Relaxation into Your Routine

To get the most benefits from relaxation, you need to integrate it into your daily routine.

We will explore how you can incorporate relaxation into your day, even when time is limited. You will learn to create unexpected relaxation moments and maintain a balance between stressful activities and moments of calm.

Practical Example: Imagine being halfway through your workday, when you usually start to feel tension and fatigue accumulating. To incorporate relaxation at this stage, you can follow these steps:

1. Planning: The evening before, plan a 15-20 minute break in the middle of your day. Ensure you have everything you need at hand: a quiet area, a comfortable chair, possibly an eye mask, or headphones with relaxing music.

2. Alarm or Reminder: Set a reminder on your phone or computer to notify you when it's time for your relaxation break.

3. Relaxation Break: When the alarm goes off, leave everything you're doing. Find your quiet spot and sit comfortably.

4. Deep Breathing: Start with some deep breaths. Inhale slowly through your nose, counting to 4, hold your breath for 4 seconds, then exhale slowly through your mouth, counting to 6. Repeat this cycle for at least 2-3 minutes.

5. Brief Meditation: If you are familiar with meditation, you can spend a few minutes on a short guided meditation. Otherwise, simply focus on your breathing and try to clear your mind of stressful thoughts.

6. Relaxing Music: If you prefer, you can listen to relaxing music during the break. Make sure it's quiet and harmonious, without distractions.

7. Light Stretching: Do some simple stretching exercises to loosen muscle tension. For example, gently rotate your shoulders, bend your neck from side to side, and do some ankle rotations.

8. Gradual Return: At the end of the break, gradually ease back into your work. Don't rush; take your time to fully wake up.

9. Monitoring Benefits: Make a brief note of how you feel after the break. Often, you will find that your mind is clearer, and you feel more relaxed, ready to tackle the rest of the day with greater efficiency. This example shows how you can incorporate a short relaxation break into your work routine. Even a few minutes of relaxation can make a significant difference in managing stress and improving productivity. You can adapt this practice to your personal needs and experiment with different relaxation techniques until you find the one that works best for you.

Chapter 9

"To successfully navigate the waters of time, it is essential to have a compass that is the measurement of your progress. Only in this way can you chart the course toward productivity and success."

The Importance of Results Measurement

The ancient adage, "what is not measured cannot be improved," is

particularly applicable to time management.

The measurement of results is the compass that guides your journey to a more efficient use of time.

Without this compass, you might find yourself adrift, with little control over the direction you are heading. That's why measuring results is fundamental to success in time management.

When you begin measuring results, you are essentially putting a magnifying glass on how you spend your time.

This may seem like a daunting prospect, but it is, in fact, extremely powerful. It allows you to see where your time is being spent productively and where you might have opportunities for improvement.

How to Evaluate Your Time Use

Evaluating your time use is like looking in the mirror for your productivity. Without careful observation, you may not notice those small details that make a difference.

Start by keeping a detailed record of your time for at least a week. Record how you spend each block of time, from the beginning of the day to the end of the evening. It will be a deep dive into your daily routine, but it will definitely be worth it.

Once you've gathered enough data, analyze it for patterns and trends. You may discover that you allocate too much time to tasks that don't contribute to your main goals or that you have peaks of productivity at certain times of the day.

This information is gold for you because it helps you identify where you can make significant improvements.

Adjust and Improve Your Planning

The real magic happens when you begin adjusting and improving your planning based on the collected information. Did you notice that the early afternoon is your peak productivity time?

Then dedicate that period to the most demanding and strategic tasks. Find that frequent interruptions disrupt your focus? Schedule dedicated break times to recharge your energy.

The key here is to make targeted and realistic changes. Don't try to completely overhaul your routine overnight. Instead, make small adjustments and continually monitor the results.

This progressive approach allows you to adapt to evolving challenges and consistently improve your time management.

Measure, evaluate, and improve.

These three steps make up the virtuous cycle of effective time management.

With regular use of this methodology, you can get the most out of every moment in your day.

Chapter 10

"Advanced time management is like navigating deep waters; it requires skill, strategy, and the ability to adapt to the ever-changing tides of life."

You have reached the crucial point of your time management journey.

You have acquired basic skills, learned to identify priorities, plan

effectively, and manage distractions.

Now it's time to tackle more complex challenges and explore advanced strategies that will take you to a higher level of efficiency and productivity. Techniques for Time Management in Complex Situations

Life often presents us with complex and unexpected situations. You may need to manage massive projects with tight deadlines or navigate multiple personal and professional responsibilities. In this chapter, you will explore advanced techniques to confidently address these challenges.

You will learn how to break colossal tasks into more manageable steps and apply time management principles to handle emergency situations. You will discover how to stay calm under pressure and maintain your productivity even when time seems scarce. Time Management in Times of Change

Life is constantly evolving, requiring flexibility in time management. You will learn how to adapt to phases of change, whether it's a new career, a move, or a shift in your personal priorities.

We will explore strategies for planning smooth transitions and making the most of the opportunities that change can offer.

This chapter will provide you with the tools to be proactive in the face of change rather than reactive, allowing you to always stay on top of your time management.

Long-Term Time Management

Time management is not just about the present but also the future. In this chapter, you will discover how to create long-term plans that will help you achieve significant goals and realize your dreams.

You will learn to establish a clear vision for your future and translate it into concrete actions.

We will explore how to balance your daily activities with your long-term aspirations and how to use strategic planning to create a meaningful life.

This chapter is the culmination of your time management journey, where your skills merge with your vision and ambition.

You will be ready to manage the present and shape the future according to your desires.

Chapter 11

" There is an old saying that goes, 'Time is money.' In challenging situations, time becomes the most precious currency we possess. Learn to invest it wisely to navigate through life's storms with determination and resilience."

How to Stay Focused and Productive in Challenging Situations

In challenging situations, the ability to stay focused and productive is crucial.

However, it can be a demanding task. Here are some strategies to help you maintain concentration and productivity:

1. Set Clear Goals: Even in difficult situations, having clear goals will give you a direction to follow. Define specific and realistic objectives that can guide you through the challenges.

2. Time Planning: Use time planning techniques, such as the Pomodoro method, to break work into focused sessions and breaks. This can help you maintain high productivity without burning out.

3. Eliminate Distractions: Identify the main sources of distraction and try to eliminate them. You may want to put your phone on silent mode or disable notifications during your work sessions.

4. Create a Conducive Environment: Ensure that you work in an organized and comfortable environment. A well-organized workspace can help you concentrate better.

5. Practice Mindfulness: Mindfulness is a technique that helps you stay in the present moment. It can assist you in managing stress and pressure, allowing you to focus better on the task at hand.

How to Manage Stress and Frustration

Difficult situations often lead to stress and frustration. Here's how to address them:

1. Acknowledge Emotions: The first step in managing stress and frustration is to recognize the emotions you're experiencing. Accept that these emotions are normal in challenging situations.

2. Stress Management: Learn stress management techniques like deep breathing, meditation, or physical exercise. These activities can help calm your mind and reduce stress.

3. Talk to Someone: Sharing your concerns with a friend, family member, or professional can be extremely beneficial. Talking about your feelings can relieve emotional tension.

4. Seek Solutions: Focus on finding solutions to problems rather than dwelling solely on the problems themselves. Problem-solving can reduce frustration.

How to Adapt Your Planning to Circumstances

In difficult situations, your planning may need adjustments. Here's how to adapt your planning to circumstances:

1. Flexibility: Be willing to change your plans as needed. Challenging situations may require adaptations, so maintain a flexible mindset.

2. Clear Priorities: Identify priority tasks and objectives and focus on them. Some tasks may need to be temporarily set aside to address more urgent challenges.

3. Communication: If you're working in a team context, maintain open and clear communication. Sharing challenges and adaptation needs can help the team collaborate better.

4. Regular Review: Regularly review your planning to ensure you stay on track. Modify deadlines or priorities as necessary, but continue monitoring your progress.

In difficult situations, time management becomes even more critical. Learning to stay focused, manage stress, and adapt your planning will help you successfully overcome challenges.

Chapter 12

" Time management within a team is like orchestrating a symphony; it requires coordination, precision, and harmony to achieve the melody of success."

In the modern world, teamwork and project management have become vital components of success in many professional fields.

In this chapter, we will explore advanced strategies for time management in a team and project context, helping you maximize efficiency and productivity.

How to define priorities and roles within a team

One of the fundamental aspects of effective time management in a team is the clear definition of priorities and roles. When each team member fully understands which activities are most crucial and what their role is in the process, it becomes easier to assign and complete tasks efficiently.

Advanced priority-setting strategies:

1. Priority Matrix: Use the Eisenhower Matrix (urgent-important matrix) to categorize tasks based on their importance and urgency. This will help establish which tasks require immediate attention and which can be flexibly scheduled.

2. Shared Goals: Ensure your team has well-defined shared goals. These goals should align with the overall project mission and contribute to its overall success.

3. Clear Roles: Clearly define the roles and responsibilities of each
team member. Ensure everyone understands their contribution to the
project and is aware of expectations.

How to plan and coordinate project activities

Planning and coordinating project activities are essential to avoid delays
and conflicts. Here are some advanced strategies to do this successfully:

1. Agile Planning: If your project is complex and dynamic, you may
adopt an Agile approach. This method involves flexible plans that
can be adapted to emerging needs.

2. Project Management Software: Use project management tools like
Trello, Asana, or Microsoft Project to assign tasks, set deadlines, and
collaboratively track progress.

3. Effective Communication: Ensure that communication is clear and
ongoing within the team. Schedule regular meetings to check
progress and address any issues promptly.

How to monitor and evaluate project progress

Project time management is not limited to the planning phase but also requires continuous monitoring. Here are some advanced strategies to do this:

1. Key Performance Indicators (KPIs): Identify KPIs that measure project success. These may include delivery times, costs, work quality, and customer satisfaction. Regularly monitor these indicators to identify any deviations from the plan.

2. Project Retrospectives: At the end of each phase or the project as a whole, conduct retrospectives. These sessions allow the team to review what went well and what can be improved for future projects.

3. Ongoing Feedback: Maintain an open feedback channel between the team and project stakeholders. Feedback can help identify issues before they become critical.

In this chapter, you have learned how to define priorities, plan projects, and monitor their progress in a team and project context.

By using these advanced strategies, you will be able to maximize your team's efficiency and ensure the success of your projects.

Time management thus becomes an essential part of achieving your professional goals.

Chapter 13

" Guard your time as the most precious treasure, for it is the foundation upon which to build a fulfilling personal life."

In today's fast-paced society, finding a balance between work challenges and personal life needs has become essential for individual well-being. In this chapter, we will delve into the realm of personal life and discover how effective time management can enhance the quality of our lives outside of work.

Finding a Balance Between Work and Personal Life

The initial challenge in time management for personal life is finding a balance between work and personal activities. Too often, work responsibilities can encroach on our leisure time, causing stress and interfering with our family and social lives. In this section, we will explore practical strategies to establish clear boundaries between work and personal life.

We will discuss the importance of taking time off to recharge and how to do so without feeling guilty. Family and social relationships are fundamental to our emotional well-being and provide emotional support.

The key to managing these commitments is planning. Begin by creating a family calendar in which you mark all important dates, such as birthdays, anniversaries, and special occasions. This will help you plan ahead and avoid scheduling conflicts.

Example 1: Imagine working in an environment where demands are constant, and you often find yourself bringing work home. To find a balance between work and personal life, you could establish a mental closing time. Decide that, unless there is a genuine emergency, work will stay at work, and you will not interrupt your dedicated family time after

6:00 PM.

Example 2: If you are a freelance professional or self-employed, you could

plan your projects so that intense deadlines do not coincide with special

moments in your personal life. For instance, avoid taking on jobs that

require significant commitment during your family vacations.

Managing Time for Recreational and Relaxation Activities

Free time is an opportunity to engage in activities that bring us joy and

satisfaction.

In this section, we will discuss how to schedule time for recreational

activities such as hobbies, sports, or simply moments of relaxation.

We will explore the importance of these activities in relaxing the mind and

reducing stress. We will also learn how to balance the time devoted to

recreational activities with other commitments.

Example 1: If you have a passion for painting, you could plan one evening

each week exclusively for painting. This can be your time for relaxation

and creativity, disconnecting from daily worries.

Example 2: If you prefer sports, you could join a soccer team or attend yoga classes once or twice a week. These regular commitments can help you maintain a fitness routine and socialize.

Planning Family and Social Commitments

Family and social relationships are cornerstones of our personal life. This section will focus on how to plan and organize family commitments, social events, and special occasions.

We will see how to manage time to maintain meaningful relationships and participate in significant events without feeling overwhelmed. We will also discuss the art of saying "no" appropriately when it is necessary to protect your personal time.

Maintaining a healthy balance between work and personal life is a challenge that requires planning and awareness. This chapter will provide you with the necessary tools to manage your time effectively, ensuring that the time spent away from work is meaningful, fulfilling, and enriching for your personal life.

Example 1: Do you have a relative's birthday party coming up, and you want to make sure you attend? Plan ahead and block that date on your calendar. This way, you avoid overlapping other commitments and ensure your time is dedicated to family.

Example 2: If you have a friend you'd like to spend more time with but are often overwhelmed with work, you could establish a recurring monthly appointment for brunch or a park walk. This creates a consistent commitment that both of you can anticipate and look forward to.

Chapter 14

"Growth is a journey that takes time, but effective time management is the key to accelerating your learning path."

Learning is a continuous process that allows us to grow and develop both personally and professionally.

In this chapter, we will explore how to use time management as a tool to optimize your learning and maximize your growth.

Setting Learning Goals The first step to effective learning is setting clear goals. Goals provide direction and purpose to your learning.

We will discuss how to identify specific, measurable, achievable, and time-bound goals (SMART goals) that will help you stay focused and motivated on your learning journey.

Identifying Specific Goals Specific goals clearly define what you want to achieve. Rather than having a generic goal like "learn a new language," you could specify wanting to "become fluent in Spanish within six months." This clarity helps you focus your efforts on what truly matters.

Measurable and Trackable Another crucial aspect of goals is that they should be measurable.

In other words, you should be able to quantify your progress. For example, if your goal is to "write a novel," you can make it measurable by setting a specific word count or number of pages to write each day or week.

Realistic and Achievable Goals should also be realistic. This means they should be attainable given your current resources, such as available time and skills.

An unrealistic goal could lead to frustration and disengagement. Therefore, it's important to be honest about your abilities and resources.

Time-Bound (SMART Goals) Another effective approach to goal setting is to use the SMART acronym, which stands for Specific, Measurable, Achievable, Relevant, and Time-bound. This methodology will help you create clear and well-defined goals.

For example, "I will learn to play a song on the guitar within three months" is a SMART goal that clearly specifies what you intend to achieve and in what timeframe.

Setting SMART goals provides you with a solid framework for your learning journey, helps you track your progress, and keeps your motivation high.

With a clear vision of your goals, you'll be better equipped to use your time effectively in learning and personal growth.

Finding Time for Study and Learning

One of the common challenges in learning is finding time to study and acquire new knowledge.

We will explore practical strategies for integrating learning into your daily routine, making use of "dead" time such as commute or lunch breaks.

You will also learn how to create a dedicated learning space and plan your study sessions efficiently.

Utilizing "Dead" Time One of the most effective ways to find time for studying is to make use of so-called "dead" time.

These are short intervals during the day when you're not doing anything particularly productive. For example, you might have free time during your commute or lunch breaks.

Using these moments to read a book, listen to an educational podcast, or take notes on your learning goals is a smart way to maximize your time.

Creating a Dedicated Learning Space Another important aspect is creating a dedicated learning space.

This can be a quiet corner in your home or a cozy spot in a local library. Ensure this space is free from distractions and comfortable. A well-organized learning environment can help you focus and adopt a positive attitude towards studying.

Planning Efficient Study Sessions Planning your study sessions is crucial for making the most of your available time. Before starting, set clear goals for what you want to achieve during that session.

For example, you could plan to read a specific number of pages in a book or complete a module of an online course.

Use tools like timers or time management apps to keep track of time and stay focused during your study session.

Maintaining Consistency Lastly, consistency is key to effective learning. Even if you have just a few minutes each day to study, maintaining a consistent routine can lead to significant results in the long run.

Consistency helps reinforce what you've learned and steadily progress toward your learning goals.

In this chapter, you'll discover how to find time for learning, no matter how busy your life is.

You'll learn to make the most of "dead" time, create an ideal study space, and plan your study sessions efficiently. Remember, learning is a valuable investment in yourself, and dedicating time to expand your knowledge will undoubtedly yield long-term benefits.

Applying Acquired Knowledge

Learning is not complete until you put into practice what you've learned. In this chapter, you'll explore how to apply your acquired knowledge in real-life situations.

We will discuss strategies for implementing your skills, using new knowledge to solve problems, and sharing what you've learned with others. You'll learn about the importance of continuous learning and how it can positively impact your personal and professional life.

Strategies for Applying Skills Putting into practice what you've learned requires action.

An effective strategy is to set application goals. After acquiring a new skill or knowledge, ask yourself how you can use it in your daily life or work. Create an action plan and commit to implementing it.

Using New Knowledge to Solve Problems The true value of your knowledge emerges when you apply it to solve problems or tackle challenges. Learn to look at situations from different perspectives and use your skills to find creative solutions. Remember that every problem is an opportunity for learning.

Sharing with Others Sharing what you've learned with others is a powerful way to reinforce your knowledge. You can do this through teaching, writing, presentations, or even casual conversations. Sharing benefits not only others but also strengthens your understanding of the material.

The Importance of Continuous Learning Knowledge is constantly evolving, so engaging in continuous learning is essential.

Maintaining an open and eager-to-learn mindset allows you to stay current with new trends and emerging opportunities. Continuous learning can enrich your life and career.

Applying what you've learned is the final step in the learning process. It turns knowledge into practical skills and real-life solutions.

By implementing these strategies, you'll not only expand your knowledge but also make a meaningful impact on your personal and professional life.

Chapter 15

"Take care of your time, take care of yourself. Well-managed time is the foundation of well-being."

How to Set Health and Wellness Goals

The first step to improving your health and well-being through time management is to establish clear and specific goals.

These goals should be realistic and tailored to your individual needs.

For example, you may set a goal to lose weight, increase your physical endurance, or reduce stress levels.

The key is to be specific and measurable in your goals. Using the SMART approach (Specific, Measurable, Achievable, Relevant, Time-bound) can help you define effective and motivating goals.

How to find time for exercise, healthy eating, and adequate sleep

Finding time to take care of your body is essential for your well-being.

You can start by planning your physical activities in advance and establishing a workout routine that fits into your daily schedule.

If possible, try to integrate physical activity into your daily routine, such as taking a walk during your lunch break or using the stairs instead of the elevator.

As for nutrition, plan your meals in advance and prepare healthy and balanced foods that you can take with you. Sleep is equally important, so try to create a regular sleep routine, avoiding nighttime distractions like electronic devices.

How to manage stress and anxiety

Stress and anxiety can have a significant impact on your health and well-being.

To effectively manage stress, it's important to practice relaxation techniques such as meditation, deep breathing, and yoga.

Additionally, learn to recognize sources of stress in your life and try to address them proactively.

Managing anxiety may also involve creating coping strategies, such as positive visualization, seeking support from friends and family, and, if necessary, consulting with a mental health professional.

Time management can help you free up time in your day for these important well-being practices.

I hope these explanations help you better understand how to manage your time to improve your health and well-being.

Chapter 16

"Time management for long-term goals is like charting a map to your

dreams. Every step you take, no matter how small it may seem, brings you

closer and closer to achieving your goals."

How to Set Realistic Long-Term Goals

The first step towards success in long-term goal time management is

setting realistic goals.

These goals should be challenging yet achievable, taking into consideration your current resources, such as time, skills, and financial resources.

Setting unrealistic goals can lead to frustration and abandonment, while reasonable goals keep you motivated.

How to Break Down Long-Term Goals into Short-Term Goals

Once you've set long-term goals, it's crucial to break them down into short-term goals. These are the smaller steps that will gradually lead you towards your long-term goal.

For example, if your long-term goal is to 'Start a business within two years,' short-term goals could include 'Choosing a business idea' or 'Researching funding options.' This breakdown makes goals more manageable and helps you track progress.

How to Monitor and Evaluate Progress Towards Goals

An essential part of long-term goal time management is the ability to monitor and evaluate progress.

Use tools like a journal or an app to record your efforts and the results achieved. This will provide you with a clear view of your advancement and help you stay motivated.

Furthermore, take the time to periodically assess whether your long-term goals remain relevant.

Circumstances can change, and you may need to adapt your goals based on new opportunities or challenges.

Time management for long-term goals requires careful planning, breaking them down into smaller goals, and ongoing progress assessment.

Chapter 17

" The key to effective time management is awareness: time is a precious gift to be invested wisely in creating a meaningful and fulfilling life."

Conclusions

You have just completed a journey through the world of effective time management. Along our path, we have explored fundamental concepts, advanced strategies, and practical applications to maximize your time and improve the quality of your life.

In this final chapter, we will summarize what you have learned and highlight the keys to effective time management. A Journey Toward Time Control

Our journey began with a simple question: "What is time?" We discovered that time is a precious, limited, and ever-evolving resource. Every minute that passes is irretrievable, so it is essential to learn how to manage this resource carefully.

We discussed the subjective perception of time and how different activities can influence our perception of time. Through the identification of priorities, we learned to distinguish between what is urgent and what is important. This understanding allowed us to set clear goals and use the Eisenhower Matrix for task prioritization.

Tools for Effective Planning

In our journey, we also examined time planning methods, from traditional notebooks to modern time management apps. We discovered how to create daily and weekly plans, using available tools to simplify this crucial task. Thanks to our exploration of sources of distraction and strategies to reduce them, we learned how to maintain focus and enter a state of flow during our most important activities. Collaborating and Maximizing Productivity

We recognized that no one can do everything alone, and the art of delegation became a crucial skill for success.

We examined modern tools that facilitate teamwork and task assignment. Personal productivity was our priority, and we explored techniques to manage time in a way that maximizes productivity.

We discovered the 2-minute rule and strategies to avoid procrastination. Balancing Work and Personal Life

Despite our quest for efficiency, we acknowledged the importance of maintaining a healthy balance between work and personal life. We learned to recognize and address stress and explored relaxation and stress management techniques that help us stay calm even in the most hectic moments.

Measuring Results and Optimization

We learned that effective time management requires continuous monitoring and evaluation of results.

We examined how to evaluate our use of time and make adjustments and improvements based on this assessment. Specific Applications

We explored how to apply time management techniques to various areas of our lives, from family and social relationships to learning and personal growth, to health and well-being.

We addressed topics such as setting specific goals, finding time for important activities, and managing stress. Long-Term Goals and the Future

We concluded our journey by adding the chapter on time management for long-term goals, exploring how to set realistic goals, break them down into short-term objectives, and monitor progress toward their achievement. The Key to Effective Time Management

Throughout our journey, we discovered that the key to effective time management is awareness. You must be aware of your time, your priorities, and your habits.

You must be willing to plan, adapt, and constantly evaluate your use of time. Time management is not a rigid formula but rather a set of adaptable principles.

You must find the strategies and habits that work best for you and tailor them to your individual needs. Time is a Gift

In conclusion, remember that time is a precious gift. How you manage this gift will directly influence the quality of your life.

With effective time management, you can free up space for what truly matters to you: time with family, pursuing your goals, taking care of yourself, and much more.

Use the knowledge and strategies you have gained in this journey to live a more meaningful, balanced, and fulfilling life. Effective time management is the key to unlocking your potential and creating the life you desire.

Thank you for accompanying us on this journey of discovering time

management. May you use this knowledge to create a future rich in

success and fulfillment.

Appendix A

Models and Examples of Weekly Planning and Activity Management

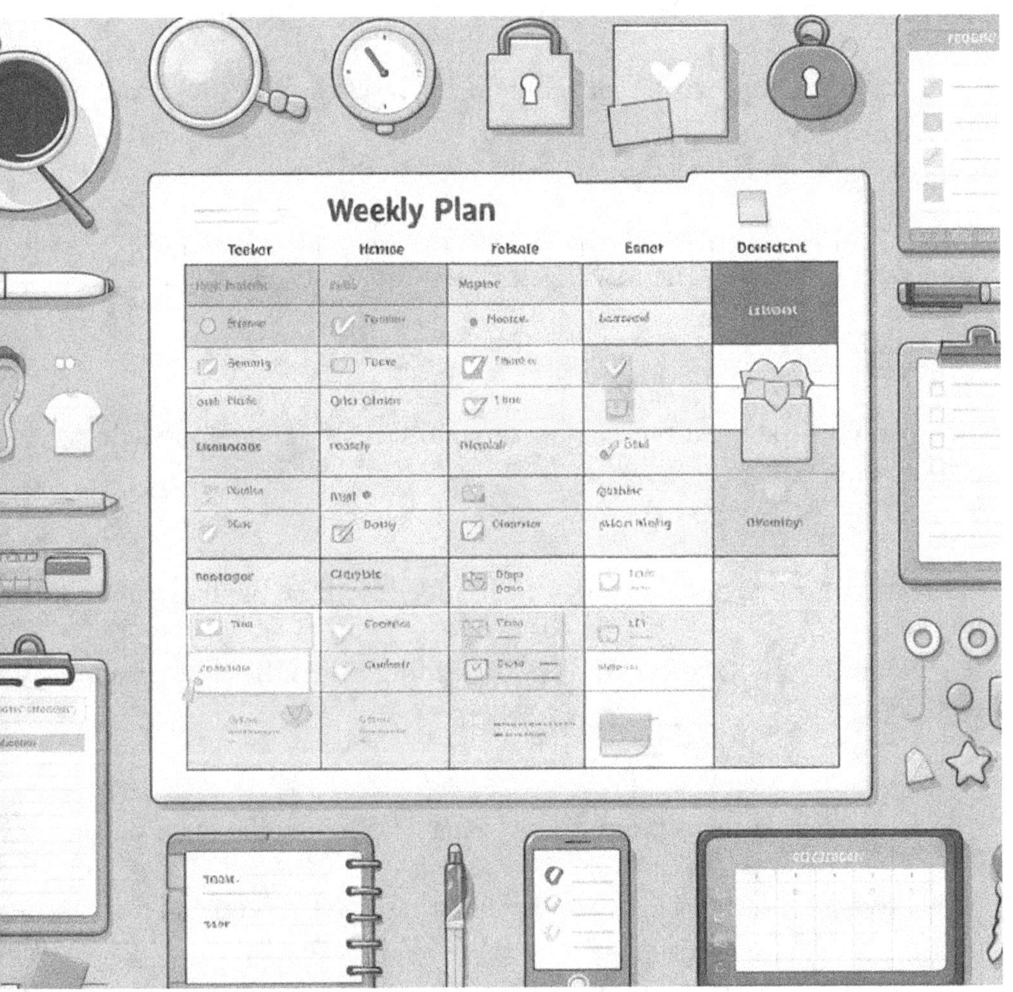

In this appendix, you will find a series of templates for weekly planning

and activity management ready to be downloaded and used. Each template is accompanied by concrete examples of how it can be filled out based on various personal or professional needs. These tools can be valuable aids in helping you organize your time effectively.

Weekly Planning Template: This weekly planning template allows you to visualize your entire week on a single page. You can download and print it or use it digitally. Here's how you can fill it out:

1. Date: Enter the reference week or specific dates at the top of the page.

2. Weekly Goals: At the top, list the main goals you want to achieve during the week.

3. Days of the Week: Each day is divided into time blocks. Enter the planned activities for each day, assigning a specific time or time range to each activity.

4. Task List: At the bottom, there is space to list all the tasks or activities you need to complete during the week. You can then assign these tasks to the appropriate days and times.

5. Additional Notes: At the end of the template, there is space for any additional notes or weekly priorities. Weekly Planning Example:

Here's an example of how you might fill out the weekly planning template: • Monday:

- 9:00 - 10:30: Work meeting

- 11:00 - 12:30: Work on Project X

- 14:00 - 15:30: Client call • Tuesday:

- 10:00 - 11:30: Project presentation

- 12:00 - 13:00: Lunch break

- 14:00 - 16:00: Work on documentation • Wednesday:

- 9:30 - 10:30: Team meeting

- 11:00 - 13:00: Data analysis

- 14:30 - 16:00: Email responses Continue to fill out the other days with your planned activities and make sure to keep it updated throughout the week. This template will help you stay in control of your time and ensure your activities are well-organized.

Task Management Template: This template is designed to help you list and manage your daily tasks. You can download and use it in paper or digital format. Here's how you can fill it out:

1. Date: Enter the date at the top of the page or at the beginning of each day.

2. Tasks: In the left column, list all the tasks or activities you need to complete during the day.

3. Priority: Assign a priority to each task, such as high, medium, or low.

4. Status: Keep track of the status of each task, such as "To Do," "In Progress," or "Completed."

5. Additional Notes: At the end of the task list, there is space for any additional notes or comments. Task Management Example: Here's an example of how you might fill out the task management template: • Date: 10/15/20XX Continue to fill out this template throughout the day, updating the status of tasks as you complete them. This will help you maintain a clear view of your priorities and tasks to be done.

Monthly Planning Template: This monthly planning template allows you to have an overview of all the events and commitments scheduled for the month. You can download and print it or use it digitally. Here's how you can fill it out:

1. Month: Enter the reference month at the top of the page.

2. Monthly Goals: At the top, list the main goals you want to achieve during the month.

3. Monthly Calendar: Each day of the month has dedicated space to enter events, commitments, and deadlines. Use different colors or symbols to distinguish between different categories of activities.

4. Additional Notes: At the end of the template, there is space for any additional notes, such as monthly priorities or important reminders. Monthly Planning Example: Here's an example of how you might fill out the monthly planning template: • Month: November 20XX • Monthly Goals:

- Complete Project X.

- Start the online time management course. Additional Notes:

- Remember the company meeting on November 10th at 3:00 PM.

- Deadline for report submission is November 25th. This template will help you plan the activities and events for the month in advance, ensuring you don't overlook any important commitments.

Priority Task List Template: This template is designed to help you focus on the most important and priority tasks. You can download and use it in paper or digital format. Here's how you can fill it out:

1. Date: Enter the date at the top of the page or at the beginning of each day.

2. Priority Tasks: In the left column, list the top 3-5 tasks that are most important for the day.

3. Priority Goals: At the end of the task list, there is space to enter the main goals you want to achieve during the day. Priority Task List Example: Here's an example of how you might fill out the priority task list template: • Date: 10/15/20XX Priority Tasks:

4. Prepare presentation for the client.

5. Complete quarterly report.

6. Resolve technical issue with the project. Priority Goals:

- Deliver the presentation by 2:00 PM.

- Complete the report by the end of the day.

- Resolve the technical issue before tomorrow's meeting. This template will help you stay focused on the most important tasks and maximize your daily productivity. I hope these additional templates are useful for you in time and activity management. You can further customize them to meet your specific needs. Happy planning!

Appendix B

Practical Exercises to Improve Time Management

In this appendix, you will find a series of practical exercises that will help

you develop and refine your time management skills.

Practicing these exercises will allow you to apply the concepts and strategies discussed in the book in a tangible way. Are you ready to get started?

1. Time Analysis: Dedicate a week to meticulously record how you spend your time. Keep a daily activity journal, noting how much time you allocate to each of them. At the end of the week, review the data and identify areas where you could improve time management.

2. Eisenhower Matrix: Use the Eisenhower Matrix to classify your tasks based on urgency and importance. Create a list of tasks and position them in the matrix. This exercise will help you focus on prioritized activities.

3. Weekly Planning: Take time every Sunday evening to plan your week. Use a weekly planning template or an app and allocate specific time to the most important tasks. Make sure to include time for yourself and relaxation.

4. Activity Rotation: When you feel tired or demotivated, try a "change of gears." Switch from one type of activity to another. If you were working on an intellectual task, dedicate time to physical or creative activity to recharge your energy.

5. Distraction Elimination: Choose a day and commit to eliminating all possible distractions. Put your phone on silent, turn off notifications, and close unnecessary browser windows. This exercise will help you discover how productive you can be when you are focused.

6. Personal Priorities: Reflect on your personal priorities and what is truly important to you. Create a list of your priorities and ensure that your daily activities reflect these values. This exercise will help you maintain a balance between work and personal life.

7. Interruption Management: Simulate real-life situations where people might interrupt you during work. For example, ask a friend or family member to "interrupt" you during a study or work session. Practice how to handle these interruptions effectively.

8. Procrastination Challenge: Identify a small task that you tend to procrastinate on and commit to completing it within a short period, such as 15 minutes. This exercise will help you overcome the tendency to procrastinate.

9. Weekly Evaluation: At the end of each week, conduct a brief assessment of how productive you have been and what you have

learned. Consider what you did well and where you could improve next week.

10. Team Time Management: If you work in a team, experiment with team time management. Organize a team meeting where you discuss how to improve planning and task distribution.